OUROBOROS

I0140164

Tom Jacobson

BROADWAY PLAY PUBLISHING INC
224 E 62nd St, NY, NY 10065
www.broadwayplaypub.com
info@broadwayplaypub.com

OUROBOROS
© Copyright 2008 by Tom Jacobson

1st printing: Dec 2008, 2nd printing: Dec 2010
I S B N: 978-0-88145-419-2

Book design: Marie Donovan
Word processing: Microsoft Word
Typographic controls: Ventura Publisher
Typeface: Palatino
Printed and bound in the U S A

OUROBOROS was produced by The Road Theater Company in North Hollywood (Producers: Shauna Bloom, Stephanie Stearns, and Kimberly Valkenaar; Executive Producer: Taylor Gilbert), opening on 20 August 2004. The cast and creative contributors were:

CATHERINE . . . . Shauna Bloom
MARGARET . . . . Taylor Gilbert
ITALIANS . . . . Josh Gordon
PHILLIP . . . . K C Marsh
TOR . . . . Paul Witten

Understudies:
CATHERINE . . . . Julie Quinn
MARGARET . . . . .Ann Noble
ITALIANS . . . . Curt Bonnem
PHILLIP . . . . John Cragen
TOR . . . . Mark Rickard

Director . . . . Michael Michetti
Assistant Director . . . . Jeff Griffith
Stage Manager . . . . .Bettina Zacar
Set design . . . . Desma Murphy
Lighting design . . . . Jeremy Pivnick
Costume design . . . . Rae Dawn Belt
Sound design . . . . David B Marling
Assistant sound design . . . . Brad Benedict
Resident vocal coach . . . . Linda de Vries
Prop designer & A S M . . . . .Randee Bayer-Spittal
Publicity . . . . Marci Hill
Photography . . . . Matt Smith

CHARACTERS

TOR, *thirty to thirty-five, handsome, blond, dresses and whistles well*

MARGARET, *forty to forty-five, attractive, blonde, repressed, dresses practically*

PHILIP, *forty to forty-five, nice-looking, dark-haired, polite, gentle*

CATHERINE, *forty to forty-five, dark-haired, very pretty, very emotional*

Italians, thirty to forty, several roles to be played by one dark, handsome, bearded actor, including:
MILANESE POLICEMAN
VENETIAN POLICEMAN
SIENESE MAN
MAN OF SORROWS
DOMINICAN MONK
MAN IN A TOWEL
GONDOLIER
PRIEST
GYPSY FORTUNETELLER
BOOKSELLER
TOUR GUIDE
SIGNOR DONNOLA

Costumes: TOR *and* MARGARET *wear warm colors, mostly yellows and golds, the brightest in Milan.* PHILIP *and* CATHERINE *wear cool colors, mostly blues and grays, the most somber in Rome.*

SETTING

The action takes place in various locations in five Italian cities. It is October.

Upstage, a curved stone wall is interrupted by two archways, one with a modern gate. Other furnishings used as needed include two chairs and a bed. The bed, if possible, should slide in and out of the upstage wall.

NOTE

The play's five sections may be performed two ways:

Rome, Siena, Florence, Venice, Milan (THE NUN'S TALE) or

Milan, Venice, Florence, Siena, Rome (THE PRIEST'S TALE)

ACT ONE

Rome

(In the darkness someone is whistling Edvard Grieg's In the Hall of the Mountain King, *which continues as the lights come up. A dark, handsome* BOOKSELLER, *thirties, hangs a banner between the two upstage arches. The banner is emblazoned with the insignia of the Roman Empire: S P Q R. The* BOOKSELLER *disappears.* MARGARET *strides on with her guidebook, stops, turns, and glares behind her.)*

MARGARET: Tor! Tor! *(Slaps her thigh)* Come on!

*(*TOR *strolls into view, still whistling.)*

MARGARET: Please stop that whistling.

TOR: *(In a Peter Lorre voice)* I can't help myself!

MARGARET: And try to keep up—you have to stride purposefully in Rome or the gypsy children will be all over you.

TOR: I'd pay for that.

MARGARET: Yes, you would. They're either incredibly subtle or incredibly vicious and— *(Pulls a money pouch from within her slacks)* —If you don't have one of these, they'll pick your pocket in a second. *(Hides the pouch again)*

TOR: I don't wanna rush my first trip to Italy.

MARGARET: That's why we're rushing—there's so much I want you to see. Bury your bitterness in art.

MARGARET:
(Looking into her guidebook)
After Sant' Ignazio and
Gesu.

TOR:
I'm not bitter.

MARGARET: Which have wonderful ceilings, I'll take you to the Pantheon, the best preserved Roman building— *(Reads from the guidebook)* "With its roof open to the heaven which gives swing to the whole."

TOR: Are we going to spend this whole trip with an illiterate guidebook?

MARGARET: Bad translation, good information. *Andiamo!* We barely have time to see all three before they close for lunch. *(Slaps her thigh)*

TOR: I'm not your basset hound.

MARGARET: At least Sophie wouldn't hang back to look available.

TOR: I saw four cute priests.

(The BOOKSELLER *appears in one of the arches, holding a book.)*

MARGARET: Please. I need to at least look like I have an escort.

TOR: I'm not your eunuch, either!

MARGARET: You're making a spectacle of yourself again.

TOR: Then stop being such a tight-ass. We're on vacation—loosen up!

MARGARET: I'm sorry. Really. *(Sotto voce)* I'd just appreciate it if you wouldn't run after everything you see in pants.

TOR: Skirts! Some naughty Roman bishop is ordaining priests for their looks.

MARGARET: *(Glancing at the* BOOKSELLER*)* Not so loud, please.

TOR: You said Italians don't know much English.

BOOKSELLER: I know a priest-a. You want to meet?

TOR: Uh...no...*grazie.*

BOOKSELLER: A book? *(Opening the one in his hands)* Past-a— *(Turning a page)* Present-a.

TOR: Look, Meg, it's Roman ruins with an overlay of how they looked new.

BOOKSELLER: Past-a—present-a!

TOR: Cool!

MARGARET: Tor, we have to hurry. *Mi dispiace.* *("I'm sorry.")*

TOR: *(As she pulls him offstage)* Yeah, sorry. Thanks. God, Meg!

BOOKSELLER: *(Hopefully)* Past-a, present-a!

(As the BOOKSELLER *disappears there is a lighting change. Almost immediately* MARGARET *and* TOR *come on, peering at the ceiling.)*

MARGARET: *(Reading from her guidebook.)* "The illusionistic decoration of the nave ceiling and dome was addled—" yes, that's what it says— *addled*— "by Il Baciccia in the seventeenth century—"

TOR: Look at all the God rays.

MARGARET: *(Reading)* "Called *The Triumph of the Name of Jesus*, this magnificently creation shows the assumption into heaven of the faithless—"

TOR. Then who arc those people falling into hell?

MARGARET: Friends of yours, no doubt. What's that in your pocket?

TOR: Meg, that's personal.

MARGARET: No it's not—it's an unnatural lump.

(TOR *pulls a votive candle from his pocket.*)

MARGARET: You're stealing candles from God.

TOR: No! They're free.

MARGARET: Did you leave an offering?

TOR: I'm supposed to?

MARGARET: Yes, and you're supposed to light it for someone's soul, not just hook it. How 'bout for Walter?

TOR: He'd like that.

MARGARET: *(Takes candle. Gets money from her pouch, gives it to him)* Put this in that slot over there. Pagan.

TOR: Am I embarrassing you?

MARGARET: No, but I'm going to take you somewhere you'll feel more at home.

TOR: A Greek temple?

MARGARET: We've been staring at ceilings and sky all morning. This afternoon we're going the opposite direction.

TOR: *(Excitedly, as he follows her out)* The catacombs? Or that chapel decorated with monkey bones?

MARGARET: Neither. And it's Capuchin *monks*, not monkeys.

(As soon as they are gone, the lighting changes and a DOMINICAN MONK *comes out of the gated entrance.* CATHERINE *drags* PHILIP *on through the ungated arch. He looks unwell, disheveled.)*

PHILIP: You don't believe a word I've said, do you?

CATHERINE: I believe every other word. Now we're going to find out about the other half. *(To the*

DOMINICAN MONK) *Quanto, per favore?* *("How much, please?")*

PHILIP: If you did, you'd understand why we can't come here—

DOMINICAN MONK: *(With an Irish accent.)* Five Euros for the two of you.

PHILIP: Catherine, it's seriously a matter of life and death—

CATHERINE: *(Handing the* DOMINICAN MONK *money.)* *Grazie.* *(To* PHILIP*)* I know that. Better than you, I'm quite certain.

*(*CATHERINE *drags* PHILIP*out through the gate.)*

DOMINICAN MONK: Don't fall on the stairs—they're dampish. *(To* TOR *and* MARGARET, *who arrive through the other arch.)* Welcome to San Clemente.

TOR: Thank you, father.

MARGARET: *(Handing the* DOMINICAN MONK *money)* He's a Dominican monk, Tor, not a priest.

TOR: Oh.

DOMINICAN MONK: *(Holding the gate open for them.)* I'm a brother. Be careful on your way down.

TOR: I always am, brother.

(Immediate lighting change as the DOMINICAN MONK *disappears after them, leaving the gate open.* PHILIP *and* CATHERINE *come in through the other archway.)*

PHILIP: I have to tell you I'm feeling very disoriented right now. I'm cold.

CATHERINE: We're fifteen feet underground. The twelfth-century nave is directly above us.

PHILIP: I wish you hadn't thrown away my map.

CATHERINE: Without a map you're less likely to stray. And I'm not afraid to ask for directions. What time is she coming?

PHILIP: She didn't give me an exact time—sometime between four and five, I think. And he's coming with her.

CATHERINE: They must have a very strange relationship.

PHILIP: She's not coming to meet me—she doesn't even know we're here. She doesn't know we exist.

CATHERINE: *(In the gated arch)* Oh, well, I have a surprise for him, too. The lowest level?

PHILIP: *(As they disappear through the arch.)* Yes. What? What surprise do you have for him? What do you have for her?

(The moment CATHERINE *and* PHILIP *disappear,* TOR *and* MARGARET *come through the other arch.)*

MARGARET: *(Reading from her guidebook)* "Around the entrance spring beautiful lovely frescoes discovered by Father Mullooly in his excavation between 1858 and 1870." That's the young boy— *(Reading from her guidebook)* —Discovered alive in the priest Saint Clement's tomb beneath the Sea of Azov.

TOR: Those priests, I tell you.

MARGARET: The church on this level was built in the fourth century, but these frescoes were added in the ninth when Pope Leo filled in between the columns to add support after the earthquake of 847.

TOR: People worshiped here? It's really creepy.

MARGARET: It wasn't underground then. And you ain't seen creepy yet. *(Pointing to the open gate)* There's another level below this one.

TOR: What's that? Cretaceous period?

MARGARET: There's a Roman altar to Mithras.

TOR: Who's that?

MARGARET: The god of an all-male religion.

(TOR *dashes through the open gate.*)

MARGARET: Tor! Oh, for heaven's sake! Tor!

(*As soon as* MARGARET *disappears after* TOR, *the lights change [becoming even spookier], and* CATHERINE *and* PHILIP *come through the ungated arch. Sounds of rushing water*)

CATHERINE: Where are they? You didn't make this up did you?

PHILIP: No.

CATHERINE: You're going to meet her later and this is some kind of dodge.

PHILIP: We probably beat them down here. Or they're somewhere off in this maze. We should leave.

CATHERINE: Let's split up—I'll go this way— (*She points.*) And you'd best call me when you find her.

PHILIP: What do you plan to do?

CATHERINE: Inspiration will strike.

PHILIP: Be careful what strikes you. You could very well lose me here.

CATHERINE: (*Just before she disappears through the gated arch.*) I've lost you already.

(CATHERINE *leaves, and* PHILIP *disappears the other way.* TOR *is heard whistling the song of the Wicked Witch of the West's soldiers from* The Wizard of Oz. MARGARET *and* TOR *come into view.* MARGARET *tries to sing along with* TOR's *whistling, but her voice cracks and sounds terrible.*)

MARGARET: Oh, dear. Even the low register.

TOR: Still gone, huh?

MARGARET: I'd hoped the trip would relax me, maybe bring it back. Oh, well. *(Reading from the guidebook, pointing)* "In the triclinium thrusts the Mithraic altar, of which around the banquet would eat to celebrate the victory of Apollo and Mithras before they ascended to heaven."

TOR: So here's where they had all-male rituals? Two stories underground?

MARGARET: Mithraism—which was really Persian, I think—valued honor and loyalty—something quite foreign to the all-male rituals you have in mind.

TOR: *(Pointing to the gated arch, which is still open)* Are those stairs? *(Peers in)*

MARGARET: That's the unexcavated fourth level.

TOR: Do they know what's down there?

MARGARET: Probably the remains of buildings burned in Nero's fire in 64 A D. But it could be Etruscan, even older.

TOR: I can't believe they haven't dug it up.

MARGARET: Probably not enough money.

TOR: The Catholic Church? More likely something they don't want people to see.

(TOR examines the gated arch more closely. Suddenly PHILIP *appears in the other archway. He and* MARGARET *see each other.)*

PHILIP: Oh.

MARGARET: Oh.

*(*CATHERINE *appears in the gated archway, almost running into* TOR.*)*

CATHERINE: Well, hello. So nice to see you both again.

TOR: Uh...nice to meet you, but—

MARGARET: I don't believe we've met. You're American?

PHILIP: *(As* CATHERINE *laughs.)* I told you they don't know us. *(To* MARGARET*)* Margaret, I know this sounds completely nuts, but you have to listen to me—

CATHERINE: No, listen to me this time—

MARGARET: How do you know my name?

PHILIP: Don't go to Milan! Promise me you won't go there.

TOR: Uh...listen—mister—you're freaking us out. At least you're freaking me out—Meg, is he freaking you out?

PHILIP: Tor, look, there's not much time, and if you care about Margaret—

TOR: Now he's really freaking me out—

MARGARET: Yes, freaking out is a pretty good description—who are you?

CATHERINE: As if you don't know! You lying cunt!

PHILIP: Catherine, shut the hell up!

MARGARET: Tor, I think—

TOR: Okay, that's enough—let's come back another time—

CATHERINE: *(Throwing herself in the archway, preventing their escape.)* No! You put me through hell—!

MARGARET: I don't know you!

CATHERINE: So it's my turn to play Virgil!

TOR: *(Starts to pull* CATHERINE *out of the way)* Out of the way, lady—

PHILIP: *(Pulling* TOR *away from* CATHERINE*)* Let go of my wife!

MARGARET: Tor!

PHILIP: I'm sorry—I'm a little desperate—we just don't have time—

TOR: What's going on?!

CATHERINE: *(To* TOR*)* You started it with your stigmata!

TOR: Stigmata!?

PHILIP: Catherine, he hasn't done that yet!

TOR: You mean like bloody palms and feet?

PHILIP: I really can't explain any of this—it's not rational—

TOR: You'd better try—

MARGARET: Tor, he's not the problem.

CATHERINE: Oh, I'm the problem? I don't think so, sister.

PHILIP: Just don't go to Milan, please!

MARGARET: But that's the whole purpose of our trip—so I can see La Scala.

TOR: It's sort of a pilgrimage—

PHILIP: It's suicide. And a sin.

MARGARET: Opera is a sin?

TOR: It depends on the production.

CATHERINE: Don't listen to him. Go to Milan. Jump off the Duomo.

MARGARET: What?

PHILIP: Catherine, she doesn't know what you're talking about. She's innocent. I'm the guilty one. The one who should be punished—

CATHERINE: Do you love my husband?

MARGARET: I don't know your husband.

CATHERINE: Philip, do you love her?

PHILIP: *(After a moment)* Yes. Yes, I have to say I do.

CATHERINE: Oh, Philip.

MARGARET: But I've never met you before.

TOR: You were right, Meg. Italy is romantic.

PHILIP: I'm sorry, Catherine, but I do love her. I love you too, but...I love her. *(To* MARGARET*)* Your thoughtfulness in Florence, your kindness to Catherine in Siena—

TOR: We haven't been to Florence or Siena!

PHILIP: But I need to know—does salvation require a leap of faith?

MARGARET: It's the grace of God, but, yes, you have to leap, I think.

PHILIP: Of course!

(Suddenly PHILIP *kisses* MARGARET.*)*

TOR: *(Pulling them apart.)* I'm gonna call a cop—if I knew Italian—

*(*MARGARET *is left gasping, but not particularly upset.)*

CATHERINE: Right in *front* of me!

PHILIP: Thank you, Margaret. You convinced me. The choice is mine, but it's the opposite of yours. We can't be together—I can't stop you from going to Milan—

CATHERINE: Thank you, Philip, for finally being honest with me. *(Starting to open her blouse)* It makes this a lot easier.

MARGARET: Excuse me, but what is easier? Nothing easy—or even comprehensible—is going on here.

CATHERINE: Look what you've done to me in the last two weeks.

PHILIP: *(Trying to stop her, but she pushes him away)* Catherine, don't show them—

CATHERINE: I'm showing you, too, Philip.

PHILIP: I deserve it, but not Margaret—

TOR: Um...lady...I'm actually mammophobic—

MARGARET: I really don't want to see—

PHILIP: Where's the light?

CATHERINE: Light, yes, that's what we need!

PHILIP: *(Stepping into one of the archways)* No, we don't! I've decided— No light!

CATHERINE: These are my wounds—but they're your scars!

(CATHERINE tears open her blouse, revealing many small scabs and wounds on her chest. Almost immediately, there is a crash from the arch where PHILIP has gone, and the lights go out completely. There is silence for a moment.)

CATHERINE: Philip? Where are you?

TOR: Meg, are you all right?

PHILIP: Catherine, give me your hand.

MARGARET: Tor, where are you?

PHILIP: Margaret, hold onto me.

CATHERINE: Philip! I feel him! He's here!

TOR: That's just me!

CATHERINE: It's him! In the dark—where he always is! I need your hand! Philip?!

PHILIP: I'm sorry, Catherine. I can't change it. There has to be a sacrifice—

CATHERINE: You can't just *decide*—

PHILIP: No greater love has any man than to lay his life down for his friends.

(There is a groaning sound from the earth, like an earthquake but somehow sentient.)

CATHERINE: Philip! No, no, please don't leave me!

TOR: Was that an earthquake?

MARGARET: Maybe, but it didn't feel exactly—

(A flashlight plays across the walls of the room from one of the archways.)

DOMINICAN MONK: *Signora e signori!* Ladies and gentlemen! *Mesdames et monsieurs! E un terremoto piccolo.* Only a small earthquake! *Uno momento! Luce! Licht!* Light!

(The lights come back on, revealing TOR *holding* MARGARET *by one hand and* CATHERINE *by the other.* PHILIP *is nowhere to be found. The* DOMINICAN MONK *comes into the room through one of the archways holding a broken light bulb.)*

DOMINICAN MONK: Is everyone all right?

CATHERINE: *(Pulling her hand from* TOR's *and hastily buttoning her blouse)* Where's my husband?

TOR: *(To* MARGARET*)* You okay?

MARGARET: Fine.

DOMINICAN MONK: This level is a labyrinth. Perhaps you can call him?

CATHERINE: Philip!

TOR: Shall we go?

MARGARET: Let's wait till she finds him. I feel somehow—

TOR: Responsible? No way!

CATHERINE: *(Disappearing into an archway)* Philip! I'm sorry! Philip!

MARGARET: Philip! *(Peering into the gated archway)* Philip!

TOR: Oh, for God's sakes, Margaret! Let's not get involved in a manhunt!

DOMINICAN MONK: Philip! *(Disappears through an arch)*

MARGARET: *(In the gated archway)* What's this? *(Kneels, picks something up)*

TOR: And don't get all archeological when we should be leaving.

MARGARET: Catherine!

TOR: Quiet!

MARGARET: That is her name, isn't it?

(CATHERINE and the DOMINICAN MONK come back through the ungated archway.)

CATHERINE: Philip?

MARGARET: Did Philip...uh...your husband—does he have an unusual wedding ring?

CATHERINE: *(Takes the ring from MARGARET)* Aah—this! *(Throws it to the floor)* Where'd you find it?

MARGARET: *(Picking it up)* Is it his?

CATHERINE: It's yours. Where was it?

MARGARET: *(Points)* Mine?

(TOR whistles the Twilight Zone *theme.)*

CATHERINE: You gave it to him. What's under here?

DOMINICAN MONK: We haven't excavated the fourth level.

(As CATHERINE starts to dig with her hands.)

DOMINICAN MONK: Ma'am, you can't do that.

CATHERINE: He's down there.

MARGARET: It's just rocks and packed debris—

CATHERINE: I heard the ground open!

TOR: That was an earthquake—we have them all the time in L A—

MARGARET: The ground doesn't just open and close without a trace—

CATHERINE: *(In tears but still digging)* Then where is he?

DOMINICAN MONK: Perhaps it's best if you leave her with me.

MARGARET: But—her husband—can't we help—?

CATHERINE: No!

MARGARET: I don't even know her and she's breaking my heart.

CATHERINE: Leave me alone!

TOR: Meg, you can't help everybody. Sometimes you lose a round.

DOMINICAN MONK: This level is closed.

CATHERINE: He's just lost.

(Lights down slowly as CATHERINE *digs and cries softly while* DOMINICAN MONK *watches.)*

CATHERINE: Very, very lost.

(Blackout)

Siena

(Offstage, TOR *whistles* That's Amore. *A* SIENESE MAN
*appears and replaces the previous banner with a Sienese Palio
[a banner awarded the winner of a bareback horse race].
As the* SIENESE MAN *leaves,* MARGARET *and* TOR *appear.*
MARGARET *wears a white alb and a wooden cross, the habit
of her order, and carries her guidebook.)*

MARGARET: Listen.

TOR: What?

MARGARET: No cars.

TOR: Very nice after Rome. The streets are too narrow
in Siena—?

MARGARET: How could they anticipate cars would be
invented six hundred years later?

TOR: Couldn't Saint Catherine have predicted it?

MARGARET: She was a saint, not a prophet. *(Points out
over audience)* See, she was holy even as a young girl.

TOR: Is that her floating up the stairs?

MARGARET: *(Pointing, then reading from her guidebook)*
And here she is— "receiving the gift of the stigmata
from the crucifix at Santa Cristina in Pisa."

TOR: Holy laser beams, Batman.

*(*TOR *makes phaser noises while holding up his hands to
receive the stigmata.)*

MARGARET: You shouldn't make fun—she's Italy's
patron saint.

TOR: So she could ruin our whole trip?

MARGARET: If we can survive Rome, we can survive
anything.

TOR: That poor woman's probably still down there digging.

MARGARET: It's sad to think our trip was just beginning when theirs was ending so badly. (*Examining the ring*) I wonder what happened to him, really.

TOR: Most likely he just left her—I would if I was married to Saint Scabby.

MARGARET: Fortunately for her, I don't think he's like you.

TOR: You're hot for him!

MARGARET: He's *married!* But do you know how long it's been since a man—an attractive man—kissed me?

TOR: I imagine your habit puts them off a bit. Or is that why you're wearing it, to catch a priest?

MARGARET: The Companion Sisterhood of Saint Gregory isn't celibate, just chaste, my effervescent sweetness, so I'm still more likely to get married than you are.

TOR: You Episcopalians find a way around anything.

MARGARET: It's my vocation!

TOR: Not an excuse?

MARGARET: For what?

TOR: Nothing. Never mind. You've always been religious—I just didn't realized you could get— *nunned*—so quickly.

MARGARET: So I'm a hypocrite?

TOR: Don't ask me—I worship all hundred and twenty-eight Egyptian gods.

MARGARET: And your gods tell you to sleep with priests? Or are you just proving all religion a fraud?

TOR: So far this trip is a great disappointment. Just a couple of pathetic wanks in the train station men's room. And these priests—oh, so attractive, and oh, so aloof.

MARGARET: Perhaps they're sincere in their vows. Imagine that.

TOR: Nah. They're definitely hypocrites—like Father Cestaro.

MARGARET: You made that up just to irritate me. There's no way he came on to you.

TOR: He did! He did!

MARGARET: Right after preaching about immorality at Walter's memorial? Not even a Jesuit is that ballsy.

TOR: "The wages of sin is death", then his hand on my ass.

MARGARET: You wish he put his hand on your ass. He's so handsome.

TOR: Did they make you vow to defend all clerics, no matter how vile?

MARGARET: What he said was reprehensible, of course—

TOR: Why else would I hate him so?

MARGARET: And if he truly touched you, you know I'd be furious—

TOR: The word of any priest over that of your erstwhile best friend—

MARGARET: Erstwhile?

TOR: Meg, why would I lie to you, of all the people in the world?

MARGARET: *(After a moment)* What a bastard!

TOR: Thank you. He said I had no appreciation for dichotomy.

MARGARET: Dichotomy? I'm so sorry, Tor. But we know he's wrong about the wages of sin.

TOR: How?

MARGARET: Walter told me.

TOR: He...you mean his...ghost?

MARGARET: No. I just didn't think you were ready to hear—

TOR: Don't protect me!

MARGARET: On his deathbed—I felt horrible being there without you—

TOR: What did he say?

MARGARET: He saw heaven. He was going there, describing it with his last breaths.

TOR: Like...what?

MARGARET: Very Hollywood, actually—clouds, God rays, the throne of judgment. I don't remember. But my point is he got there.

TOR: Meg, the nurse told me he went out screaming.

(MARGARET *looks away.*)

TOR: What did he see?

MARGARET: Nothing.

TOR: That's why you stopped singing.

MARGARET: Tor, please. I know you're trying to be a good friend, but I don't need adult supervision.

TOR: *(Trying to change the tone)* You did when I pried that Philip guy off you after he started haunching on your leg.

MARGARET: *(Laughing and looking at the ring on her finger)* It was a very nice kiss. Here's what came with it.

TOR: *(Looking at it)* A snake swallowing its own tail. And why are we wearing it?

MARGARET: *(Shrugs)* I know. A Bride of Christ shouldn't be thinking about other men.

TOR: Another romance with a dead man.

MARGARET: That's about my speed. Shall we float up the street to see Saint Catherine's relics?

(TOR puts his arm around her and whistles Some Enchanted Evening *as they leave. Lighting change as* CATHERINE *and* PHILIP *enter with a map. He looks somewhat disheveled.)*

PHILIP: I just don't get this map. I can't find north.

CATHERINE: Perhaps, darling, you're insufficiently medieval.

PHILIP: Or perhaps it's because I didn't want to come here. I didn't get lost in Venice, and that was much more complicated.

(CATHERINE snorts.)

PHILIP: What? I didn't.

CATHERINE: Didn't what?

PHILIP: Get lost. This is the first time this vacation my sense of direction's failed me.

CATHERINE: You seemed to have some difficulty finding your way back to our hotel the night you chased after the ghost woman.

PHILIP: You sent me after her! We had a very long, very heated conversation. I told you that.

CATHERINE: Heat!

PHILIP: She had some strange ideas.

CATHERINE: Did you sleep with her?

(PHILIP *just stares at* CATHERINE. *She pulls out a ring.*)

CATHERINE: Why did you keep her ring?

PHILIP: I threw that away this morning in Florence!
Get rid of it!

CATHERINE: I found it in the wastebasket in our hotel.
Did you sleep with her?

PHILIP: Yes.

CATHERINE: Whose strange idea was that?

PHILIP: Catherine, I'm really, really sorry. I've been so
anxious, I'm practically sick. I didn't intend to tell you
like this—wait till the trip was over so you wouldn't
get—so it wouldn't—

CATHERINE: Wouldn't get what? Dangerous? Unstable?
But then I just wouldn't be me, would I?

PHILIP: I've never done anything like this before and
I never will again. I'm supposed to protect you, not—
but I've never lied to you. I could have lied just now—

CATHERINE: I'm sorry, I'm not giving out extra credit
points. Who is she and why did you do it? Why this
time and never before? I've been worse before—I've
driven you away before—why now?

PHILIP: She told me something.

CATHERINE: She loves you. She said that in Milan when
we first saw her.

PHILIP: Yes—

(CATHERINE *snorts.*)

PHILIP: —But that's not the extraordinary part. She told me I loved her. I don't, of course, but she says I told her that in Rome.

CATHERINE: You've never been to Rome. You won't be in Rome until the day after tomorrow.

PHILIP: Exactly.

CATHERINE: Are you always attracted to women with mental problems?

PHILIP: She had this theory. It's alchemy. And it has to do with this ring. *(He takes the ring.)*

CATHERINE: That's why you kept it?

PHILIP: It's the symbol for this alchemical process—and we're stuck in it. It's circular, goes backwards and forwards at the same time, always striving for balance. Maybe this is my punishment, my judgment—maybe some kind of sacrifice is required to offset—

CATHERINE: You're leaving me!

PHILIP: No! You know I can't!

CATHERINE: She's more interestingly insane than I am! You have this urge to nurture—

PHILIP: I'd never want to leave you!

CATHERINE: You did that night!

PHILIP: And if I did, it wouldn't be for someone else! Only if I thought it best for you. Maybe I'm your problem.

CATHERINE: I need to pray. I'm feeling rather vengeful right now.

PHILIP: I'll pray with you. *(Kneels)* We can do it right here.

CATHERINE: No, we're trying to find San Domenico—we might as well—

(A SIENESE MAN walks by.)

CATHERINE: *Scusi, Signore. Dov'e la chiesa di San Domenico? ("Where is the church of Saint Dominic?")*

SIENESE MAN: *(Points through archway) Eccola, Signora! Eccola qua! ("There it is, Signora! It's there!")*

CATHERINE: *Mille grazie. ("A thousand thanks.")*

(The SIENESE MAN leaves.)

CATHERINE: It's right there. Maybe Saint Catherine can help.

(PHILIP and CATHERINE leave through the archway. Lighting change as the SIENESE MAN sets two chairs upstage between the arches, then disappears as MARGARET and TOR appear. They stare at something out over the audience.)

TOR: Now that's barbaric.

MARGARET: It's a great honor. Preserved relics have tremendous spiritual power.

TOR: Good thing I'll never be a saint.

MARGARET: Did I ever tell you my favorite story about Saint Catherine?

TOR: We didn't get to that chapter of Martyrdom Bedtime Tales.

MARGARET: She was nursing wounded soldiers and found herself nauseated by the blood and suffering. So to overcome her disgust, she drank a bowl of cancerous pus.

TOR: They didn't have Alka-Seltzer in those days?

MARGARET: She was extreme, but that's how you end up with an altar dedicated to your memory.

TOR: *(Referring to the altar)* It's so ghoulish. Do you think the gift shop has a postcard of this?

MARGARET: I'm sure they do.

(MARGARET *and* TOR *exit.* CATHERINE *drags* PHILIP *on.*)

CATHERINE: Her altar should be right over here.

PHILIP: Catherine, please—

CATHERINE: This is why we had to come to Siena instead of Arezzo—

(*They look where* TOR *and* MARGARET *had been looking.*)

CATHERINE: It's...my head!

PHILIP: It's Saint Catherine's head.

CATHERINE: I'm Catherine.

PHILIP: You're not a saint.

CATHERINE: I'm looking into my own face!

PHILIP: Sweetheart, that head's been dead six hundred years. See, it's all dried up, yellow—

CATHERINE: It's like a mirror!

PHILIP: Catherine, please. It's just a relic—

CATHERINE: It means I'm going to lose my head!

PHILIP: (*Leading her to the chairs*) You lose your head every day. You always get it back.

CATHERINE: Philip, I feel it—I'm going to—

PHILIP: (*Setting her down*) No. No, don't start—

(CATHERINE *scratches furiously at her chest and arms.*)

PHILIP: —No! No scratching!

(PHILIP *grabs* CATHERINE'*s hands. She pulls free and keeps scratching.*)

PHILIP: Catherine, stop it!

CATHERINE: I can't stop! That's my head!

PHILIP: Okay. That's it. I'm calling a cab and we're going back to the hotel. Can you wait here for a minute?

CATHERINE: They took my head!

PHILIP: I'll just be gone a second. Try to relax, calm down. Do your—I know!—do your visualization exercise.

CATHERINE: I can't visualize without my head!

PHILIP: *(Holding her)* Think of Jesus. Come on, you know this works. The Good Shepherd who loves you.

CATHERINE: *(Stops scratching)* Jesus...

PHILIP: *(Kissing and stroking her)* Close your eyes and think of Jesus. He's coming to comfort you. Everything will be all right.

CATHERINE: *(Relaxing somewhat, her eyes closed)* Jesus...yes...I'm trying.

PHILIP: Good. Jesus will be here with you while I go get a cab. Then we'll go back to the hotel and watch C N N.

CATHERINE: Jesus. I think He's coming.

PHILIP: *(Stepping away from her)* Just relax and think of Him and I'll be back before you know it.

CATHERINE: Please, Jesus...

(PHILIP *dashes out. Almost immediately, the* MAN OF SORROWS *appears, the crucified Christ, with bloody hands, feet and side. He wears only a loin cloth and crown of thorns.)*

CATHERINE: I know you love me. Your sufferings were for me. Please come. Let me see you. Oh, Lord, please. *(She opens her eyes and sees him. She gasps.)* Thank you. I knew you'd come. But you're not the Good Shepherd. You're the Man of Sorrows. Why are you so sad? Is it sin? The sins of the world you sacrificed your life to save? Or is it me? Are you sad for me?

(MAN OF SORROWS *nods, sadly.*)

CATHERINE: You *are* sad for me! You know—of course, you know! You know more than I do! It's my sin that makes you sad? My husband's sin? Or both?

(MAN OF SORROWS *smiles, suddenly looking devilish rather than holy.*)

CATHERINE: It is! It's our sin! But why are you smiling? You're smiling at our sin! Only the Devil smiles at sin! *(Gasps)* You're not Christ at all! You're him—you're Evil! Disguised as Jesus! Are you here to take me away? To take my husband? Go away! Get thee behind me!

(MAN OF SORROWS *starts to laugh, cruelly.*)

CATHERINE: Oh, Jesus—the real Jesus!—save me! *(Buries her face in her hands)* Help!

(MARGARET *and* TOR *appear but cannot see the* MAN OF SORROWS. MARGARET *hands postcards and a votive candle to* TOR *and goes to* CATHERINE, *putting her arm around her.*)

CATHERINE: Oh, Jesus, help me, please!

MARGARET: Shhh! It's all right. It's all right. Jesus is here. He's always here.

CATHERINE: *(Trembling violently)* Satan is here!

MARGARET: This is a church. A holy place.

CATHERINE: He's everywhere.

(MAN OF SORROWS *kisses* TOR *on the cheek [which* TOR *does not notice] and leaves.*)

MARGARET: But so is God. And God's more powerful.

CATHERINE: How do you know?

MARGARET: I have special connections.

CATHERINE: Who are you?

MARGARET: I'm Sister Margaret Mary.

(CATHERINE *looks up for the first time. All three of them gasp.*)

TOR: Meg, it's Saint Scabby!

CATHERINE: My husband is fucking *a nun*!

TOR: No, he's not. She's only a postulant. And he's not fucking her. She decided to be a nun right after she read the letters of Abelard and Heloise. Of course, Heloise was a nun who has an affair with a priest, but that's *not* why Meg became a nun, cause the priest ended up castrated as punishment—

MARGARET: Tor, those aren't exactly words of comfort—

TOR: And anyway your husband's dead or sucked down to hell or something—

(PHILIP *comes in.* MARGARET *and* TOR *both gasp.*)

PHILIP: I got the cab—

(PHILIP *sees* MARGARET *with her arm around* CATHERINE, *comforting her.*)

CATHERINE: My husband is a minister.

PHILIP: Margaret.

CATHERINE: A Lutheran minister. Which is why you'd think he'd feel more guilt.

MARGARET: Guilt, for what?

PHILIP: Lutheran guilt is very bad.

TOR: Worse than Catholic guilt? Or Jewish guilt?

PHILIP: Yes, because we also feel guilty for not being Jewish or Catholic.

CATHERINE: No one's laughing, Philip. (*To the others*) I'm Catholic.

TOR: *Quel surprise.*

PHILIP: We weren't gonna come to Siena. Couldn't talk her out of it—Catherine wanted to see her saint. *(To* MARGARET*)* And I'm glad to see you. I shouldn't be, but I am. I can't help it.

MARGARET: Why?

PHILIP: Margaret, she knows. I told her.

MARGARET: *I* don't know.

PHILIP: But I can't leave her. She needs me.

CATHERINE: And I'm Catholic. Don't forget that, Philip. No divorce!

PHILIP: I thought I could fix things if I never saw you again, get our life back to normal—but now that we're here maybe I can warn you, convince you—

TOR: Don't start with that "Beware the Ides of Milan" shit again.

MARGARET: Tor. *(To* PHILIP*)* I just want to go to La Scala. I used to be a singer—

TOR: And I conduct— *(Conducts)* —She's in my choir—

MARGARET:	TOR:
Was. But I'm becoming a teacher and this is kind of my farewell to performing—	She's retiring, to put it bluntly.

PHILIP: You're performing at La Scala? You didn't tell me that.

MARGARET: Oh, no.

CATHERINE: My husband is fucking the Singing Nun.

MARGARET: I can't sing any more.

TOR: She lost her voice. Post-traumatic whatchamacallit. We're in Italy to bury ourselves in culture before she abandons Los Angeles for Pennsylvania—she's a little depressed and can't forgive God—

CATHERINE: God can't forgive *her*.

TOR: But he ought to 'cause he needs forgiveness, too. It's reciprocal, don'tcha think?

MARGARET: Tor! Please don't babble.

TOR: Sorry.

PHILIP: Unless we do something, you'll die, too, just like Signor Donnola in Florence—

MARGARET: Die, how?

CATHERINE: Suicide! I recommend it. Although I've never been able to get it right.

TOR: You're the one who died or disappeared or whatever.

CATHERINE: Where?

MARGARET & TOR: In Rome.

CATHERINE: We haven't been to Rome.

MARGARET: Yes, you have. Three days ago.

PHILIP: What was the date?

TOR: The twelfth of October.

MARGARET: No, I think it was the thirteenth. We left L A on the twelfth.

TOR: That's right.

PHILIP: We were in Milan on the thirteenth.

CATHERINE: And so were you!

TOR: No, we weren't!

PHILIP: Okay, okay. What day is today?

TOR: *(Looking at his watch. Outside, the cab honks.)* The seventeenth.

CATHERINE: Your watch is wrong.

PHILIP: It's the twenty-fourth. We were in Venice on the seventeenth.

CATHERINE: And so were you!

PHILIP: Today's the twenty-fourth for us, and the seventeenth for you.

TOR: Um...excuse me, but, one day at a time, I think, is how it works.

PHILIP: Let's ask a third party.

(They look around, see no one. PHILIP starts to leave.)

PHILIP: The cab driver.

CATHERINE: Oh, Philip, you don't know enough Italian. *(She goes.)*

MARGARET: Is she gonna be all right?

PHILIP: I don't know what happens to her. I only know what happens to you and me if we don't change things.

TOR: What things? What should we change?

MARGARET: Are you talking about the future?

PHILIP: The future and the past.

(They just look at him.)

PHILIP: We're caught in something together, some kind of time thing—it might be called an Ouroboros, I don't know. And I'm trying to change it, change our itineraries, change something—

TOR: This is ridiculous.

PHILIP: Then how do you explain that I know you're gay?

TOR: And I thought I was so butch.

PHILIP: And that you want to sleep with priests.

TOR: Oh, who doesn't?

PHILIP: And that you think Margaret is in love with you. Margaret told me that.

TOR: Meg!

MARGARET: I did not!

PHILIP: In Venice.

MARGARET & TOR: We haven't been to Venice!

PHILIP: And Margaret isn't in love with you. She's in love with me.

MARGARET: I am not!

(CATHERINE *comes in, but* PHILIP *doesn't see her right away.*)

PHILIP: We made love in your hotel room in Venice.

CATHERINE: The cabbie agrees with me. It's the twenty-fourth. He showed me his watch.

TOR: No way! (*He runs out.*)

MARGARET: We did not make love. I never slept with your husband.

CATHERINE: I wish I believed you.

PHILIP: We did. We did.

MARGARET: Okay, prove it. If we made love—which we have not—what's my orgasm like? What do I do?

PHILIP: You...cry. You sob. You burst into tears.

(*They all stare at each other.* TOR *comes in.*)

TOR: He showed me his watch. It's the seventeenth.

MARGARET: Tor, we need to go.

TOR: But I just proved them wrong—

MARGARET: (*Dragging him out the door*) We need to go *now!*

PHILIP: *(As they disappear)* Margaret, I'm sorry!

(Sound of cab driving off. PHILIP *looks at* CATHERINE.*)*

PHILIP: Very, very sorry.

CATHERINE: You should be. They've taken our cab.

*(*CATHERINE *leaves.* PHILIP *follows.)*

Florence

(Offstage, TOR *whistles* Toccata and Fugue in D Minor.
A TOUR GUIDE *appears, removes any other props, and
installs a railing near the back wall, then changes banners;
the new one has a representation of Michelangelo's* David.
TOR *appears and leans against the railing, whistling.
He is studying the unseen upper portion of the opposite wall.
After a moment,* CATHERINE *appears. They see each other
and he stops whistling.)*

CATHERINE: *(Peering over the railing)* Oh, it's so high!

TOR: *(Gesturing toward the opposite wall)* Look up at the
devils instead.

CATHERINE: Is my husband among them?

TOR: Probably. Eventually. Have you seen Meg? I'm
pretty sure she said she'd meet me up here in the dome.

CATHERINE: I haven't seen your wife since my husband
disappeared after her in Venice.

TOR: She's not my wife. And we haven't been to Venice.

CATHERINE: Oh. But this *is* Florence, right?

TOR: Yes.

CATHERINE: The only Duomo with so many devils in
the dome.

(They lean against the rail together, staring at the Last
Judgment *fresco on the opposite wall.* TOR *whistles* The

Theme from Vertigo. MARGARET *and* PHILIP *appear and almost run into each other across the stage from* CATHERINE *and* TOR, *who do not see them [and vice versa].* MARGARET *wears her traveling clothes.*)

MARGARET: (*Shoving a votive candle into her purse*)
Oh, dear.

PHILIP: Oh, my. I'm...I'm supposed to meet my wife under the dome.

MARGARET: Tor is supposed to be here, too, but who knows where he is. (*Awkward pause. She looks down.*) Amazing floor, huh?

PHILIP: Yes. If Catherine were here, she could tell us all about it. She's an art historian.

MARGARET: Ah. I have to apologize for my behavior in Siena.

PHILIP: Too bad we're not going there so I'll never know what you mean.

MARGARET: I freaked when you told me we made love in Venice.

PHILIP: I'm really, really sorry. It was a terrible mistake.

MARGARET: Telling me?

PHILIP: No, what we did in Venice. Poor Catherine waited up half the night. And she's not very well.

MARGARET: I'm sorry, too. I feel awful for her.

PHILIP: I've been almost sick about it myself. But... it wasn't bad—

MARGARET: —For a nun.

PHILIP: You're a nun? I'm going to hell.

MARGARET: You saw what I was wearing in Siena.

PHILIP: No. It's not on our itinerary.

MARGARET: Our itinerary is Rome, Siena, Florence, Venice, and Milan.

PHILIP: Ours is Milan, Venice, Florence, Arezzo and Rome. Then the fun ends and we go to Limoges.

MARGARET: So we didn't see each other four days ago in Siena?

PHILIP: What's today?

PHILIP & MARGARET: October twenty-first?

MARGARET: Oh, that's good. I think. Maybe things are normal now.

PHILIP: No, I don't think so. We're right in the middle of our trip and so are you.

MARGARET: Oh, my. A whadyacallit—

PHILIP: A palindrome.

MARGARET: Able was I ere I saw Elba?

PHILIP: *(Holding out his hand, which she shakes.)* Madam, I'm Adam.

MARGARET: But you're not...in love with me, are you?

PHILIP: No. I'm sorry.

MARGARET: No, that's good, cause I'm not in love with you—it's just that—

MARGARET & PHILIP: You said you were in love with me in Rome/Milan.

(MARGARET and PHILIP laugh.)

MARGARET: What else do I do in Milan?

PHILIP: You ask me about the pain of sacrifice—no—martyrdom. Why it's better than the pain of life.

MARGARET: What do you say?

PHILIP: I'd...rather not tell you. I think it's what makes you jump off the roof of the Duomo.

MARGARET: Unlikely.

PHILIP: Then you float off into the sky.

MARGARET: With God rays and an angel chorus just like a Counter-Reformation ceiling?

PHILIP: Well...yes. And what happens to me in Rome?

MARGARET: I'm not sure. You disappeared in the lowest level of San Clemente and your wife seemed convinced the earth had opened up and swallowed you like Faust.

PHILIP: She has these night terrors—

MARGARET: Do you pray?

PHILIP: Professionally.

MARGARET: Oh, that's right. Me, too. I'm very confused—would you pray with me while we wait for the people we're supposed to be with?

PHILIP: How odd. We've spent most of this trip in churches and I haven't talked to God in any of them.

MARGARET: Then I think we ought to.

(MARGARET *and* PHILIP *kneel and pray silently together.*)

CATHERINE: How lovely to actually spend time looking at a single work of art! I never get to do this any more. Notice the symmetry of the four large devils north, south, east and west. I've forgotten their names, probably Asmodeus, Beelzebub—but the interesting thing is the symmetry. As the Middle Ages were giving way to the Renaissance, the symmetry is still there, but it's more dynamic—you know, the Golden Mean— and the figures are more realistically human—or in this Last Judgment, demonic— *(Looks down)* There he is!

TOR: Beelzebub or Asmodeus?

CATHERINE: My husband. With her! *(Cups her hands to her mouth to holler)*

TOR: *(Grabbing her hands)* Rather than make a spectacle of yourself, why don't we see if they do?

CATHERINE: What an evil notion. I think I like you after all.

(CATHERINE *and* TOR *lean over the railing to watch as* MARGARET *and* PHILIP *conclude their prayer and stand.*)

MARGARET: Your wife seems to be an intensely emotional person.

PHILIP: What a gentle way to put it.

MARGARET: Do you think she'll go through the roof if she finds us looking at the side chapels together while we wait?

PHILIP: Probably. But she doesn't know what happened in Venice.

MARGARET: Yes, she does. You told her in Siena.

PHILIP: Oh, my. Another reason not to go there.

CATHERINE: *(Peering over the railing as* MARGARET *and* PHILIP *gaze at the walls.)* They're just looking at the art.

TOR: She can't very well blow him in the sanctuary.

CATHERINE: I blew him in the sanctuary once, back home.

TOR: That's right. I forgot he's a minister.

MARGARET: By the way, I have your ring.

PHILIP: I know. And I have yours.

MARGARET: You do?

PHILIP: *(Taking it out)* We compared them in Venice. They're identical. You left it with me when you ascended in Milan.

MARGARET: *(Taking out her ring)* When you disappeared in Rome, this is all that was left.

PHILIP: So you got the ring from me and I got the ring from you?

MARGARET: I guess that's right.

PHILIP: Then where did it come from? Who bought it?

PHILIP & MARGARET: I didn't.

MARGARET: Not only does this thing that can't exist exist, there are two of them.

(MARGARET reaches out to take PHILIP's ring.)

PHILIP: No, don't. Maybe they shouldn't touch— like matter and anti-matter.

(PHILIP and MARGARET laugh.)

CATHERINE: Wait a minute, how do you know he's a minister?

TOR: You told me in Siena.

CATHERINE: Hmm. Well, he's a very good one, at any rate. Even if his church is dying. There are too many Lutheran churches in Chicago, so Philip only has old people. They love him, of course—he's the care-giving type.

TOR: I imagine so.

CATHERINE: Is that a crack? I think that was a crack. But it's true. Always saving everybody but himself. He takes good care of me and I'm profoundly depressing. His life is full of disappointments. I keep telling myself that's why he's sparkin' with your wife.

TOR: Sparkin'?

PHILIP: I know we're trying to avoid saying this, but something very strange is definitely going on here and we haven't been taking it at all seriously.

MARGARET: Okay, if our trips are the reverse but somehow simultaneous in this kind of palindrome and you know what happens in Milan and Venice and I know what happens in Rome and Siena, who knows what happens here in Florence? I don't.

PHILIP: Me, either. So for the rest of my trip I'll know more and more about you, and you'll know less and less about me?

MARGARET: And vice versa.

PHILIP: How sad.

MARGARET: It's an experiment in predestination!

PHILIP: Except that here—in Florence where neither of us knows what will happen—we're free.

MARGARET: *(Touches him to stop him walking.)* So what we do here, while we're free, is our only chance to change the future—or the past—whichever—

CATHERINE: I'm on anti-depressants.

PHILIP: *(Taking MARGARET's hand, excitedly)* Which means we can surrender to this thing—whatever it is—or thwart it—only here in Florence.

CATHERINE: And they're not working!

MARGARET: Tell me everything about Milan and Venice and I'll tell you everything we did in Rome and Siena, down to the minute.

(PHILIP and MARGARET leave.)

CATHERINE: Is that Paolo and Francesca?

TOR: Who? I don't think I can handle running into someone else I know.

CATHERINE: See that couple flying through the air of Hades locked in eternal coitus? I'm sure that's Paolo and Francesca from Dante's *Inferno*—they were murdered adulterers.

(CATHERINE *begins to scratch herself rather vigorously.* TOR *grabs her hand.*)

TOR: (*Grabbing her hand as* CATHERINE *starts to scratch herself.*) Please don't do that—it's horrible.

CATHERINE: I have an itch!

TOR: You have dozens of disgusting scabs and sores across your chest.

(CATHERINE *is aghast.*)

TOR: You showed them to me in Rome.

CATHERINE: I never show anyone. Not even my husband if I can help it.

TOR: Is it some kind of compulsive thing?

CATHERINE: I pick. For the last fifteen years. I've seen a lot of doctors about it, but I can't stop.

(CATHERINE *to do it again, but* TOR *grabs her hand.*)

TOR: You're not gonna do it in front of me.

CATHERINE: Like you should talk, with your stigmata!

TOR: You said that in Rome. What stigmata?

CATHERINE: In Milan you showed everyone your wounds like some kind of Catholic tourist attraction!

TOR: (*Showing her his palms*) I don't have wounds!

CATHERINE: You did!

TOR: This trip is a nightmare. Meg and I are trying to relax—recover from—well, a lot of things, but we keep running into you weird—aggressively weird—people, Meg's getting weird, too—unpredictable—and I haven't gotten laid the whole time I've been in Italy.

CATHERINE: Oh, shut up! Do you have any idea how long it's been since I've had sex?

TOR: That's different—you're married! All these gorgeous priests in all these churches and—nothing! I want to get fucked so hard my foot goes numb and I limp for three days! *(Starts to leave, turns back)* And you can tell Meg that's what I'm doing when you go down there.

(MARGARET and PHILIP can be heard singing offstage.)

CATHERINE: *(As TOR disappears.)* I'm not going down there! *(Turns and peers over the railing, scratching)* I can't go down there.

PHILIP & MARGARET: *(Entering quietly singing* Lord of All Hopefulness.*)*
Be there at our sleeping, and give us, we pray
Your peace in our hearts Lord, at the end of the day.

MARGARET: That's my favorite hymn.

PHILIP: Really? Mine, too. My parishioners love it, so I put it in the bulletin almost every month.

MARGARET: It's so sweet and sad. *(Gasps)*

PHILIP: Do you see Catherine?

MARGARET: I was singing! I haven't been able to for six months!

PHILIP: You did in Venice.

MARGARET: Oh, thank you!

PHILIP: Catherine and I used to sing together.

MARGARET: You made me forget I couldn't.

PHILIP: Oh, my. I just realized the only time this phenomenon becomes apparent is when I see you. If we didn't keep running into each other, Catherine and I would just go on with our trip, on with our lives, and we'd never know the difference.

MARGARET: That's true. It only involves the four of us. The rest of the world just blithely passes by.

PHILIP: That's one way to stop it, then. Avoiding each other.

MARGARET: Which should be easy, since you plan to go to Arezzo instead of Siena.

PHILIP: Oh, that's right. Good.

MARGARET: You could even change your plans and avoid Rome.

PHILIP: Catherine would be disappointed.

MARGARET: I would be too if I didn't go to Milan.

(CATHERINE *is joined by a handsome* TOUR GUIDE *wearing a long coat, who peers over the railing next to her. Lights come up dimly inside one of the archways.*)

PHILIP: *(Playing with his ring)* Or we could throw these away.

MARGARET: Wouldn't you rather figure this out than just run away from it? I'm dying of curiosity. Don't you want to know what's happening to us?

PHILIP: Yes, but I'm concerned—

MARGARET: If the rings are important, then let's ask somebody about them—a museum or a jeweler or something.

PHILIP: Museums don't just evaluate things like that— Catherine sometimes has expertise day at the Art Institute, but you can't just walk in—

MARGARET: *(Thumbing through her guidebook)* Okay, a jeweler, then.

PHILIP: Are there jewelers in your guidebook?

MARGARET: There's all kinds of obscure information, amusingly translated from Italian.

PHILIP: *(Pulling out a map)* We get by with maps. Catherine knows what everything is, but I have to get us there.

MARGARET: *(Reading)* "The old Ponte Vecchio bridge is the most elderly bridge over the Arno. Goldsmiths ply their lustrous trade upon it, some quite unusual and rare. Reject them all but Signor Donnola, for only he has what your heart desires." Sounds like a kickback from Signor Donnola to me. Let's go.

PHILIP: I should wait for Catherine.

MARGARET: And I should wait for Tor. But they both should have been here half an hour ago. Maybe they ran off together.

PHILIP: Maybe Catherine decided to take a nap. I'll call the hotel.

MARGARET: Don't be pussy-whipped.

PHILIP: You are a most unusual nun.

MARGARET: According to you, I even fly.

(MARGARET and PHILIP leave. CATHERINE scratches more violently.)

TOUR GUIDE: *Lei e sola, Signorina?*

CATHERINE: Oh, yes, I'm alone.

(Behind them in the archway, TOR saunters past wearing nothing but a white towel. He disappears.)

TOUR GUIDE: You're American! You are so beautiful, I thought you were Italian.

CATHERINE: *(Stares at him a moment)* My grandparents were from Caserta. Weren't you in Milan a few days ago?

TOUR GUIDE: *(Gestures toward the fresco)* No. You appreciate saints. Do you like relics?

CATHERINE: I am a relic.

TOUR GUIDE: I show you bones of amazement.

CATHERINE: Your line is dreadful, but your timing— *(Glances over the railing.)* —Is impeccable.

(CATHERINE and TOUR GUIDE leave together. Lighting change. PHILIP and MARGARET appear, consulting his map.)

PHILIP: This is the Ponte Vecchio, so Signor Donnola should be there—through that arch—

MARGARET: I've got this weird feeling about Signor Donnola. I've heard his name before.

(Behind them, in one of the archways, TOR and another MAN IN A TOWEL appear from different directions and size each other up, almost mirroring each others' movements. After a moment, they put their hands under each other's towels, then start making out.)

MARGARET: What if trying to figure this phenomenon out is what actually causes it?

PHILIP: So we're punished for our curiosity?

MARGARET: Or rewarded with a spiritual gift.

PHILIP: That sounds so New Agey—God handing out merit badges.

MARGARET: I'd like to think I had some hand in my own fate.

PHILIP: Does fate hinge on a single act or a series of decisions?

MARGARET: Either way you're hauled before the throne of judgment.

PHILIP: And condemned.

MARGARET: Or forgiven.

PHILIP: Do you think this phenomenon is Christian?

MARGARET: If Christianity can encompass resurrections and healings and stigmata, why not this?

PHILIP: But who believes in those kinds of miracles these days?

MARGARET: I do.

PHILIP: Catherine does.

MARGARET: Sometimes I think we make God too small.

PHILIP: *(Gesturing to the archway)* Then let's go see how big he is.

(PHILIP, MARGARET, TOR and the MAN disappear as CATHERINE appears.)

TOUR GUIDE: *(Off)* Signora, come here! I have fingers, thighs, hair—

CATHERINE: *(Engrossed in unseen reliquaries)* In a minute. Here's another fragment of the True Cross, and *la spina*—another thorn from the Crown of Thorns— I think I've seen enough to make a whole briar patch. I can't tell you how grateful I am you brought me here— these reliquaries are wonderfully gruesome, and I was just in the mood. I feel the suffering of the saints so personally sometimes.

(CATHERINE continues to peruse the reliquaries on one side of the stage, while MARGARET and PHILIP follow SIGNOR DONNOLA on from one of the archways. He is dressed as a shopkeeper and carries one of the rings.)

SIGNOR DONNOLA: *Questo anello é maledetto.*

MARGARET: Excuse me, not everyone speaks—

SIGNOR DONNOLA: *(Fairly strong Italian accent)* Ring is cursed. Where you get?

MARGARET: He gave it to me.

SIGNOR DONNOLA: And where you get?

PHILIP: She gave it to me.

SIGNOR DONNOLA: *(Rolls his eyes)* The legend say who possess the Ouroboros find what heart desires.

MARGARET: Isn't that a blessing, rather than a curse?

PHILIP: I suppose it depends on what's in your heart. What did you call it?

SIGNOR DONNOLA: Ouroboros—the dragon devouring his own tail. In alchemy the symbol for cycles, eternally round and round. With every turn pure elements rise, base ones sink, refining closer and closer to perfection.

MARGARET: Can it turn lead to gold?

SIGNOR DONNOLA: No one knows—alchemists who make disappear in fifteenth century. Rings, too. There were two. So I must tell you ring is false. Legend say are together or not at all.

PHILIP: *(Producing the other ring)* Then I must tell you it's true.

SIGNOR DONNOLA: Let me see.

PHILIP: Who were the alchemists?

SIGNOR DONNOLA: I don't know names. One in Roma and other in Milano. Please.

PHILIP: *(Reluctantly handing him the ring)* Are they gold?

SIGNOR DONNOLA: Oh, no. That I can tell you just by eye. *(Holding them next to each other, but not touching them together.)* Also same mold mark, this little flaw. Mass produced, I am sure.

PHILIP: I'm not so sure.

SIGNOR DONNOLA: I tell you what. I call expert friend. *Uno momento. (Disappears through an archway with the rings)*

MARGARET: You don't trust him, do you?

PHILIP: Neither do you. *Maledetto!*

SIGNOR DONNOLA: *(Recorded. Offstage as* MARGARET *and* PHILIP *talk.) Avvoltoio? Qui Donnola. Non puoi imaginare cio che ho in mano. Gl'ourobori— Esattamente come gli anelli tutt'e due. Si, un dragone che si mangia la coda. Esattamente come la foto del mille ottocento ottante cinque. É come se fossero caduti nelle mie mani—un regalo dal cielo. Questi turisti. Schiocchi Americani—non hanno alcun'idea. Ah, si, possono sentirmi ma non capiscono l'italiano. Certo che sono d'oro fino. Ma tu sai che valgono piu del metallo in se. Qualsiasi museo pagherebbe un patrimonio. Un migliardario pagherebbe anche di piu. Infatti credo che dobbiamo venderli privatamente or saremo nei guai con il governo. Certo che conto su di te! Sei il mio esperto—come posso venderli senza di te? Nessuno mi creder senza qualche autorité. E tu sei legato alle persone piu ripugnanti—no, sto scherzando! Ma ovviamente questa situazione molto delicata e no mi serve solo il migliore. Certo che ti lusingo! Ma non ho bisogno di farlo, no? Sei tanto entusiasmo quanto me. Non si vedono questi anelli da piu di cent'anni—non credevo veramente che esistessero. Perche sono proprio uguali— fino all'incavo vicino alla testa del drago. Gli ho detto che era un'impronta dalla forma. É da ridere, no? Sono cos creduloni. Ho l'intenzione di dire a loro che li prender per dieci Euro, come curiosite. Ho bisogno del tuo aiuto. Vieni qui e digli che sono solamente bagatelle. La maledizione? Ma non esiste. É stato creata per spaventare la gente. Sono assolutamente squisiti e non ti devo dire quanto pregiati. Vieni adesso! Se posso ottenere questi anelli, muoio come uomo beato. Ciao! ("Avvoltoio? It's Donnola. You won't believe what I have. The Ouroboros—both rings. Yes, a dragon devouring itself—both of them. Just like the photograph from 1885. It's like they just dropped into my hands—a gift from heaven. These tourists. Stupid Americans—they have no idea. Oh, they can hear me, but they speak no Italian. Of course they're real gold. But you know as well as I do they're worth more than just the metal. Any museum would pay a fortune. Private investors would pay more. In fact, I think we have to go private or the government will be on our backs. Of course I'm counting you in! You're my expert—how can I sell them without you? No one will believe me without some higher authority. And you have the most unsavory connections— I'm just joking! But this is obviously a most delicate situation and that's why I need the best. Of course I'm flattering you! But I don't need to, do I? You're as excited as I am. These rings haven't been seen for more than a hundred years— I didn't really believe they existed. Because they're exactly alike—down to a dent near the dragon's head. I told them it was a mold mark. Isn't that funny? They are so gullible. I'm going to tell them I'll take them off their hands for ten Euros, just as curiosities. I need your help. Come over and tell them they're just trinkets. Curse? There's no such thing! Someone just made that up to scare people away. They're absolutely beautiful and I don't have to tell you how valuable. Come over now! If I can get these rings, I'll die a happy man. Ciao!")*

MARGARET: *(Continuing over* SIGNOR DONNOLA*)* I wish I could remember where I heard his name.

PHILIP: He's just jabbering away in there. Can you understand any of it?

MARGARET: He's going awfully fast.

PHILIP: If he offers to buy them, we'll just say no.

MARGARET: Shhhh!

(As MARGARET *and* PHILIP *listen intently to* SIGNOR DONNOLA's *conversation,* TOR *and* MAN IN A TOWELL *appear in the dimly lit doorway. They are still wearing towels and have their hands all over each other.)*

TOR: *(Whispering)* I wish I knew how to say "condom" in Italian.

MAN IN A TOWELL: *(American accent)* I think it's *preservativo.*

TOR: You're American!

MAN IN A TOWELL: But I don't have a condom.

TOR: They gotta have 'em up front. Maybe at that espresso bar thingie.

MAN IN A TOWELL: Let's go.

CATHERINE: Luca, come see this. Tell me if you think it's real. Luca?

(MAN IN A TOWELL and TOR come out of the archway into brighter light. CATHERINE disappears into the other archway.)

MAN: *(Staring at TOR revealed in light)* Oh, my God! Tor!

TOR: Father Cestaro!

FATHER CESTARO: What are you doing in Florence? I haven't seen you since the funeral.

TOR: You hypocritical fuck! The wages of sin!

(TOR suddenly slugs FATHER CESTARO and runs out. FATHER CESTARO recovers, then runs out after him.)

FATHER CESTARO: *(As he disappears)* Tor! You asshole! You still don't understand dichotomy!

MARGARET: Philip, I believe he's trying to cheat us.

PHILIP: What'd he say?

MARGARET: He's called us names more than once. And he's using a lot of money words. Something about the government. Sounds like he's trying to get someone to help him. He's really buttering him up. This guy is an incredible sleaze!

PHILIP: Should I just take the rings so we can get out of here? Catherine must be going crazy.

MARGARET: No, I'll enjoy telling him we're onto him.

PHILIP: Now what's he—?

MARGARET: Shhh!

CATHERINE: *(Off.)* Luca, I think it's Saint Catherine of Siena—part of her, rather.

(CATHERINE comes into view, with the TOUR GUIDE following. She points.)

CATHERINE: She's my absolute favorite saint. I'm named after her cause I was born on her day. What do you think that is? The label's handwritten in that old style—

TOUR GUIDE: Is toe.

CATHERINE: Saint Catherine's toe. I can't tell you how much I identify with her—kind of a mystical connection.

TOUR GUIDE: Been to Siena?

CATHERINE: No, and unfortunately it's not on our itinerary this time.

TOUR GUIDE: If you love Santa Caterina, you visit birthplace. And San Domenico.

CATHERINE: What's there?

TOUR GUIDE: Is very holy.

CATHERINE: I could use a little holiness, but we're going to Arezzo and my husband wouldn't want to change plans—

TOUR GUIDE: Italy is for changing plans. Come—I show you shroud of Caterina.

(CATHERINE and the TOUR GUIDE go back through the arch.)

MARGARET: He's going to offer us ten Euros.

PHILIP: That's just a few dollars!

(MARGARET *suddenly gasps.*)

PHILIP: What? What did he say?

MARGARET: I just remembered who told me his name.

PHILIP: Who?

MARGARET: You. In Siena. We have to get out of here.

PHILIP: Not without our rings.

MARGARET: You told me he died.

PHILIP: Oh. Well, we'll just have to make sure he doesn't, which will put an end to this whole Ouroboros thing.

MARGARET: We can't play with a man's life—

PHILIP: *(Grabs her)* We're not! Margaret, nothing is going to happen! You're acting just like my wife! Yes, odd things have been going on, but only between you and me. And I don't want to give that up. *(Embarrassed, he lets her go.)* I mean, you're a very nice nun—and I'd like to—you know—stay on your Christmas list after we all go back to our lives.

MARGARET: But what if it's immutable and we never go back to our lives?

PHILIP: We'll change it.

SIGNOR DONNOLA: *(Returning with a ring in each hand)* I am sorry. Signor Avvoltoio agrees my opinion, but will come prove worthlessness of these rings. I feel bad, so I pay you ten Euros for them for your trouble.

PHILIP: Ten Euros!

SIGNOR DONNOLA: Each.

MARGARET: *Lei un imbroglione e un bugiardo! ("You are a liar and a cheat!")*

SIGNOR DONNOLA: *Anche Lei, che fai finta di non capire l'italiano! ("So are you, pretending not to know Italian!")*

PHILIP: *(Holding out his hand for the rings)* Give us our rings and we'll be leaving.

SIGNOR DONNOLA: No, no—stay until Signor Avvoltoio comes. You believe him.

MARGARET: You lied about the mold marks and everything.

SIGNOR DONNOLA: Your wife is very...American. Skeptical. Is not becoming in woman. *(Holding the rings together to show them.)* Molded, not original. See, hold them together— *(He gasps.)* Insieme— *("Together—") (Drops the rings and stumbles backward, clutching his heart.)* Il cuore! *("My heart!")*

MARGARET: Philip, it's happening!

PHILIP: No, we can save him! *(Catching* SIGNOR DONNOLA *as he falls.)* Signor Donnola—is it your heart? Isn't that what he said—heart?

MARGARET: He touched them together! *(Falls to her knees to retrieve the rings, one in each hand.)*

PHILIP: Then don't you touch them! Call 9-1-1! Do they have 9-1-1 in Italy?

*(*PHILIP *attempts mouth-to-mouth for* SIGNOR DONOLLA*.)*

MARGARET: There's nothing we can do. It's fate. Or maybe our judgment.

*(*TOR *runs out on stage through an archway, still in his towel. He stands there, trembling with anger.)*

PHILIP: Get rid of the rings—it's the only way to stop this! Margaret, please—call the police! This man has no pulse whatsoever!

CATHERINE: *(Running back out of the archway to stare at the reliquary.) Uno momento,* Luca! One last look at Saint Catherine's toe.

TOR: Of all the people in the world—!

CATHERINE: Yes, a mystical connection.

MARGARET: It's too late, Philip.

PHILIP: Not if we never see each other again.

CATHERINE: Catherine, I need you. We're coming to Siena.

(PHILIP *pounds helplessly on* SIGNOR DONNOLA's *chest.* MARGARET *clutches a ring in one hand, and presses the other into* PHILIP's *hand. They stare at each other. The lights fade.)*

END OF ACT ONE

ACT TWO

Venice

(Offstage TOR *whistles* O Solo Mio *or some other tune frequently sung by gondoliers. A* VENETIAN POLICEMAN *appears and changes banners to one featuring a winged lion [the symbol for Saint Mark and Venice]. Then he pulls out a bed upstage center and leaves.* CATHERINE *and* PHILIP *appear, gazing over the audience.)*

CATHERINE: Venice traded extensively with the East, so these Doomsday mosaics derive from the Byzantine rather than Roman tradition.

PHILIP: The skulls with the worms in the eyes are certainly gruesome.

CATHERINE: Aren't they compelling? They almost seem like contemporary art.

PHILIP: Too compelling. Hell's so fascinating heaven looks dull. I guess that's true of any Last Judgment.

CATHERINE: You're always intrigued by lost souls. Paintings of Lot's wife, Jezebel, Judas—

PHILIP: Shall we go? *(Taking out his map)* At least I won't get lost. I can even read this upside down.

CATHERINE: Philip, you're a very bad tourist. Everyone gets lost in Venice. That's the point of Venice.

PHILIP: We don't have time to get lost.

CATHERINE: There's something innately depressing about being a tourist. You know you're only seeing the surface of everything, never going any deeper. All we saw in Milan was *The Last Supper* and the Duomo.

PHILIP: We saw quite a bit more in Milan than your average tourist, if you count jet-lag hallucinations.

CATHERINE: Next flight, no melatonin. I think it clashed with my medication.

PHILIP: I wish we could find out what really happened to that poor woman.

(Offstage, TOR *whistles* Chain Gang.*)*

CATHERINE: I tried, darling. I'm sorry my Italian isn't any better.

PHILIP: You're right—surface! This bizarre thing happened and we don't know why.

CATHERINE: Even in our everyday life it's no better. We never know much.

PHILIP: I suppose if we did, we'd be God.

*(*MARGARET *and* TOR *appear,* TOR *still whistling.* CATHERINE *and* PHILIP *continue to gaze. Neither couple sees the other.)*

MARGARET: My dear, it's really rather tasteless to whistle while crossing the Bridge of Sighs.

TOR: We're going to a prison. It's a prison tune.

MARGARET: The last thing my life needs is underscoring.

TOR: It's already got great locations and special effects. Look at all this tagging.

MARGARET: You've lived in L A too long. This graffiti is the tragic outpouring of souls surrendering to their fate.

TOR: Is that what you want to do?

MARGARET: Surrender to my fate?

TOR: You believe all this crap, don't you? You like it, even! Despite what happened in Florence—no!—*because of* what happened in Florence—!

MARGARET: If you'd been there, you'd understand.

TOR: I was! Running into Father Cestaro was a disgusting coincidence, but won't change my life.

MARGARET: What I witnessed was horrifying. There is no comparison.

TOR: So this Midwestern soothsayer makes a bunch of predictions and one of them comes true—

MARGARET: An absolutely awful one!

TOR: That doesn't mean time is going backward—

MARGARET: It's not going backward. It's going forward, just in different directions for different people.

CATHERINE: Here I am, a so-called expert—*the* expert in Limoges enamels since Jacques Marandel died—and I still have everything to learn about those stupid fucking plates. I'll die a dilettante.

PHILIP: Those plates got you a free flight to Europe.

CATHERINE: Somebody at the Art Institute has to write this catalogue or we have to give the enamels back to the donor.

PHILIP: It's a compliment! When was the last time they asked an editor to actually write—?

CATHERINE: They're just tossing me crumbs because they don't care enough to hire a real curator. It's humiliating to have to write a book no one will read.

TOR: Meg, should I be worried?

MARGARET: About what?

TOR: That our trip to Milan is going to end with a self-fulfilling prophecy?

(MARGARET *doesn't answer.* TOR *starts whistling* Que Sera Sera.)

PHILIP: *(Taking* CATHERINE's *hand, comfortingly)* You're a real curator to me. A Renaissance woman.

CATHERINE: And therefore totally unemployable in the twenty-first century. The woman who knew too much.

(CATHERINE *and* PHILIP *leave through one of the archways.)*

MARGARET: You know I hate that song.

TOR: Prophecies are usually wrong. Saint Scabby said I would get stigmata— *(Holds out his palms)* —And look, no chocolate mess!

MARGARET: You simply don't understand faith.

TOR: Faith!? You wanna find him here in Venice, don't you?

(MARGARET *glares at him a moment, then disappears through an archway.* TOR *follows.* CATHERINE *and* PHILIP *sit on a gondola bench, with a* GONDOLIER *piloting the boat behind them with his pole.)*

CATHERINE: You know, if my husband got stigmata, I'd jump off the Duomo, too.

PHILIP: Why?

CATHERINE: Envy. As a child I always felt cheated that all the miracles happened so long ago. People in the Bible got special tutoring in faith and I was left to fend for myself. Plus I identify with saints. Saint Catherine of Siena, of course, and there was one—I forget the name—who mortified his flesh by picking at his scabs, never letting them heal.

PHILIP: It's nice we're here in October, when it's not so crowded. Aren't you glad we splurged on a gondola?

CATHERINE: Sometime on this trip you're going to have to deal with me, Philip.

PHILIP: What?

CATHERINE: I'm here so I can go to Limoges and research those disgusting enamels, but you're along—

PHILIP: To see Europe for the first time.

CATHERINE: —So we can explore some things.

PHILIP: So—explore.

CATHERINE: This isn't about weaning me off my medication. It's not even about being turned down for adoption.

PHILIP: *(Standing)* Is this our stop?

GONDOLIER: *Si, Signore.*

PHILIP: You're—we're—not stable enough for kids anyway.

CATHERINE: *(Standing)* Exactly. It's about divorce.

(CATHERINE and PHILIP leave through an archway as MARGARET comes in through another, pursued by TOR's whistle.)

MARGARET: *(Slapping her thigh)* Tor, come on!

TOR: *(Calling from offstage)* Quit skittering ahead— what are you looking for?

MARGARET: *(Consults her watch anxiously, smiles slyly, then calls off.)* Tenente! Tenente, ho bisogno di aiuto. *("Officer! Officer, I need some help.")*

VENETIAN POLICEMAN: *(Appearing)* Si, Signora?

MARGARET: *Quell'uomo mi segue da piu di mezz'ora. ("That man's been following me for over half an hour.")*

(TOR appears, still whistling.)

VENETIAN POLICEMAN: *E un complimento alla Sua bellezza. ("It is a compliment to your beauty.")*

TOR: Are we lost? Are you asking directions?

MARGARET: *Mi fa paura. Per favore, gli chieda di smettere. ("He's frightening me. Please ask him to stop.")*

VENETIAN POLICEMAN: *Come vuole, Signora. ("As you wish, Signora." To* TOR*) Vada a seguire un'altra signora. ("Go follow another lady.")*

TOR: I'm sorry. I don't speak Italian. Meg, what did you tell him?

VENETIAN POLICEMAN: *(Pushing* TOR*) Non discuta. Si muova! ("Don't argue, just move along.")*

TOR: Hey! Meg! Tell him I'm okay!

VENETIAN POLICEMAN: *Va via! ("Go away!")*

TOR: *(Desperately trying to communicate by means of signs.)* I know her! I came here with her!

MARGARET: *Dice che mi vuole violentare! ("He's saying he wants to rape me!")*

VENETIAN POLICEMAN: *(Grabbing* TOR*) Giochi sono giochi ma non scherziamo. Dovrò arrestarLa? ("Fun is fun, but let's not take it too far. Am I going to have to arrest you?")*

MARGARET: I told him you want to rape me.

TOR: I'm going to be arrested for your fantasies!?

VENETIAN POLICEMAN: *Smetta di essere volgare con lei! ("Stop speaking filth to her!")*

MARGARET: *Va bene, tenente. È mio marito. ("It's all right, officer. He's my husband.")*

VENETIAN POLICEMAN: *(Taking his hands off* TOR. *To* TOR*) Castrato! (To* MARGARET*) Troia! ("Slut!") (Leaves in disgust)*

TOR: How'd you get him to lay off?

MARGARET: *(Grinning)* I told him you were my husband.

TOR: You told me this trip would change me, but suddenly you're lying to cops and chasing men. You're mutating before my eyes!

MARGARET: My dear, green is not your color.

TOR: I'm not jealous—you're crazy. You want to sleep with this guy just because he told you you would!

MARGARET: Yes, I do! I do want to make love with him!

TOR: Really? I was only speculating. What about his wife? Doesn't she count?

MARGARET: I feel sorry for them both. They're pulling each other down. She needs to be free of him, too.

TOR: And that's your job?

MARGARET: I have always done what my parents wanted me to do, what my teachers wanted, my employers—you! I'm old enough to do what I want for the first time in my life. I'm too old to do anything else!

TOR: What about what God wants? What about breaking holy vows?

MARGARET: Who are you to talk about God?

TOR: You're not fighting with me, you're fighting with Him.

MARGARET: Maybe He likes to be fought with. Remember Jacob wrestling with the angel? A little resistance, a little *thinking!* Maybe God approves of this whole thing.

TOR: I guess when you jump off the Duomo, we'll know if he approves.

*(*MARGARET *just glares.)*

TOR: I'm only saying don't get reckless just cause you're disappointed by life. You used to be so risk-averse.

MARGARET: Disappointed by life?

TOR: Life. Love.

MARGARET: How astonishingly arrogant to think I'm unhappy because I'm not like you.

TOR: Why do you think I'm going into debt for this trip? To protect you from yourself—I can't lose you, too!

MARGARET: Lose me?!

TOR: You lost your voice. For weeks you didn't get out of bed.

MARGARET: I was reading!

TOR: Abelard and Heloise, yes, I know.

MARGARET: People deal with trauma differently.

TOR: I dealt with it alone. When you finally do show up, you're moving to Pennsylvania, going into seclusion, *retiring*. You plunged into religion to get away from me—

MARGARET: I was called! I had no choice!

TOR: —That's hypocrisy worse than Father Cestaro—!

MARGARET: I'm not in love with you!

TOR: I'm disappointed, too. I'd like not to be making my living writing grants to finance other people's creativity! I'd prefer not to be conducting a rinky-dink community choir full of bad singers! And I *really* wish the man I've loved for seven years was here with me. Now you're leaving me, too. I am desperately disappointed, but I'm not committing suicide!

MARGARET: Your whole life is suicide.

TOR: Whoa! My life or my *lifestyle*?

MARGARET: Suicidal because *you're* the one who thinks you're bad. The wages of sin. Walter wasn't your fault. He just had to go.

(TOR *starts to leave.*)

MARGARET: Where are you going?

TOR: To find someone to help me slit my wrists.

MARGARET: Does that mean I have the hotel room to myself tonight?

TOR: Oh, yes.

(TOR *leaves.* MARGARET *lets out a sigh, then consults her watch. She peers into an archway, then darts into the other one. After a moment,* CATHERINE *and* PHILIP *appear through the first archway.*)

CATHERINE: My needs always come first—it's time we thought about yours.

PHILIP: This is not the self-sacrifice decathlon.

CATHERINE: I could never compete with you in that. We need to explore—

(CATHERINE *is trying to take the map from him;* PHILIP *keeps it.*)

CATHERINE: —Go off the goddam map.

PHILIP: I'm not—rigid. Don't you love me anymore?

CATHERINE: Frankly, it's the opposite.

PHILIP: You think I don't love you?

CATHERINE: Oh, darling, how could you possibly?

MARGARET: (*Crossing through and disappearing through an arch.*) Hello, Catherine. Hello, Philip.

PHILIP: Oh, my.

CATHERINE: A vision! An apparition! Go after her.

PHILIP: Come with me.

CATHERINE: Go beneath the surface of her mystery. Explore. Ask her back to the hotel. I'll meet you there.

PHILIP: We only have one map.

CATHERINE: I want to get lost.

(PHILIP *hesitates.*)

CATHERINE: Go.

(PHILIP *disappears through the archway after* MARGARET. CATHERINE *heaves a sigh, then leaves another way. Lighting change focuses on the bed and a nearby collection of votive candles.* MARGARET *comes in with* PHILIP.)

PHILIP: May I use your phone to call my wife?

MARGARET: Oh, this won't take long. The ring's right here.

(*As* MARGARET *pulls it from under the bed,* PHILIP *reaches for it.*)

MARGARET: No, we can't let them touch, believe me. Hold yours up.

(PHILIP *does.* MARGARET *holds hers about a foot away from it.*)

MARGARET: See, identical. Down to that flaw, that nick. They're the exact same object. The snake swallowing its tail.

PHILIP: I got mine from you. Where did you get yours?

MARGARET: From you.

PHILIP: Oh, no. I've only seen you—

MARGARET & PHILIP: —Once before.

MARGARET: I know. But I've seen you three times before. (*She lights the votive candles.*) Every time I did,

I bought a candle. I thought they were for a friend,
but I guess they're for you.

PHILIP: You've been spying on me—us?

(MARGARET *laughs. Dimly lit in one of the archways,*
TOR *appears with a* PRIEST. *The* PRIEST *carries a large
cross and leans it against the wall inside the arch.*)

PRIEST: *Spogliati! ("Take off your clothes.")*

TOR: I'm sorry, I don't speak—

(*The* PRIEST *rips opens* TOR' *shirt.* TOR *gets the idea and
disrobes.*)

MARGARET: We don't have much time. I'd rather not
waste it explaining.

PHILIP: Then I need to get back to my hotel—my wife—

MARGARET: You're going to see me three more times,
but I'm only going to see you once more.

PHILIP: How can that be?

MARGARET: *(Coming very close to him)* God. I think. I'm
pretty sure it's God. You're a minister—you tell me.

PHILIP: How do you know I'm a minister?

MARGARET: Your wife told me.

PRIEST: *Sbrigati! ("Hurry up!")*

PHILIP: Catherine isn't in on this. If you know I'm a
minister—and you know Catherine—then you know
why I need to leave now.

MARGARET: Not yet. I like that you're a minister.
I researched the other owners of these rings—all
monks, priests, and nuns—from the middle ages
to 1885. We're like Abelard and Heloise.

PHILIP: Who are they?

MARGARET: I'll tell you later. No—Tor will. In Siena.

PRIEST: *Christi eleison.*

*(*PRIEST *ties* TOR *to the cross.)*

PHILIP: In Milan you said you loved me. I don't love you.

MARGARET: You will.

PHILIP: I don't know you. We have nothing in common.

MARGARET: We've both sacrificed ourselves because we think we don't deserve love. All my life I've surrounded myself with the wrong men—too young, too attractive, too—

PHILIP: Too nuts. Pardon me for saying so, but your husband *undressed* on top of the Duomo.

MARGARET: My husband? *(She laughs.)* Oh, Tor, I can't wait.

PHILIP: And speaking of him, aren't you breaking some vows just by having me here?

MARGARET: As a matter of fact, yes, but some vows are best broken.

(Once TOR *is tied to the cross, the* PRIEST *lights a cigarette and stares at him, smoking. As the* PRIEST *lights his cigarette,* MARGARET *extinguishes one of the votive candles.)*

MARGARET: For instance, your vows to Catherine.

PHILIP: I have never been unfaithful to my wife. You are amazingly confident.

MARGARET: You're still here.

PHILIP: *(Starts to leave through an arch)* You're right. I can't blame this on anyone but myself.

MARGARET: She's not going to divorce you, if that's what you're worried about.

PHILIP: You couldn't possibly know about that.
She brought it up for the first time today.

MARGARET: I also know she's attempted suicide—
more than once, it sounded like.

PHILIP: She—*we*—had an abortion fifteen years ago,
before we were married. It messed her up inside—
(Gestures to his abdomen, then his head) —And inside—

MARGARET: I've never been exactly suicidal, but ask Tor
about my month in bed, my flight to Pennsylvania—

PHILIP: We applied for adoption, but Catherine's
medicated, so—

(The PRIEST, *still smoking, caresses* TOR *all over.* TOR *gazes
heavenward and whistles* Rock of Ages.*)*

MARGARET: She's eating you alive.

*(*PHILIP *sits down on the bed.* MARGARET *puts out another
candle.)*

MARGARET: On this trip, every time I see frescoes of
martyrdom, I think of you. I'm afraid that's your heart's
desire—suffering for others, suffering for some cause—
you have to stop punishing yourself—

PHILIP: I'm...Lutheran.

*(*MARGARET *and* PHILIP *both laugh.)*

MARGARET: We have suffering in common. You're
married to a woman who has visions of Satan. I've been
in love with a man whose goal is to sleep with a priest.

PHILIP: Your husband?

MARGARET: My friend. My amazingly loyal friend.

PHILIP: Are you still in love with him?

MARGARET: He thinks so, but no, not since...not any
more. Do you love Catherine, or is it just sacrifice?

PHILIP: There's love...and there's love.

MARGARET: Six months ago, a friend of mine saw heaven. Just like a bad Charleton Heston movie—mist, bright light, and in the distance, the throne of judgment. As he got closer, he got very excited—he was going to see God. The throne was simple, magnificent—and empty. No judge. No God. He started screaming and wouldn't stop. Faced with emptiness, a moral void, I lost faith, lost my voice. Finding you is like finding faith again.

PHILIP: That wasn't really heaven. There's no empty throne.

MARGARET: I keep hoping there's a reason it's empty. A good reason.

PHILIP: Don't tell me there's no judge.

(MARGARET *begins to brush her hair, gazing into a mirror.* CATHERINE *appears from the other archway, wearing a nightgown, mirroring* MARGARET's *actions.*)

MARGARET: There must be, otherwise why the throne? *(Looking into the mirror)* Ah!

PHILIP: What? Who?

MARGARET: *(With sudden astonishment)* Right in front of me!

(MARGARET *smiles and sings along with* TOR's *whistling.*)

MARGARET: Rock of ages, cleft for me
Let me hide myself in thee

(CATHERINE *joins* MARGARET *in song as they let down their hair while gazing at each other in invisible mirrors. They harmonize.*)

CATHERINE & MARGARET: *(Oblivious to each other except as reflections)*

Let the water and the blood
From thy riven side which flowed

(PHILIP *joins them in harmony.* TOR *continues to whistle.)*

CATHERINE, MARGARET & PHILIP:
Be of sin the double cure
Take my guilt and make me pure

PHILIP: Catherine and I used to harmonize like that.

(MARGARET *kisses* PHILIP. *He does not resist.)*

PHILIP: How did you know I'd stay?

MARGARET: You told me.

(MARGARET *puts out the last candle, plunging the bed into darkness. In the darkness, the bed disappears from the stage.)*

PRIEST: No one forgets their first trip to Italy.

TOR: You speak English!

PRIEST: Or their last.

(PRIEST *burns* TOR'*s palm with the cigarette.)*

TOR: No, no, don't!

(*Blackout on* TOR *and the* PRIEST*)*

CATHERINE: *(Still gazing in the "mirror".)* Saint Catherine, watch over my husband this night. Protect him from—

(CATHERINE *stops as she hears the sound of* MARGARET *sobbing in the darkness. Blackout)*

Milan

(A Gypsy FORTUNETELLER *posts a banner depicting*
Leonardo da Vinci's Last Supper. PHILIP *leads* CATHERINE
on through an archway.)

CATHERINE: *(Laughing)* No, Philip—it's too touristy!

PHILIP: Don't be such a tight-ass!

FORTUNETELLER: *La bella fortuna!* I tell future! *Signore,*
Signora—the desire of your heart!

CATHERINE: Mine is to take a nap! Come on, Philip.

PHILIP: No, we have to stay up to avoid jet lag. We're
still flying! How much for two? Due?

CATHERINE: *(Sighs) Quanto per due fortune, Signore?*

FORTUNETELLER: Ten Euros.

PHILIP: *(Handing him money)* Oh, see, Catherine,
it's cheap.

FORTUNETELLER: Each.

CATHERINE: That's outrageous!

PHILIP: *(Handing him more money)* Don't you want to
know how our trip will go? *(To the* FORTUNETELLER*)*
Tell us about the next two weeks—beyond that I don't
care. *(Holds out his palm)*

FORTUNETELLER: No read hand. God write fortune.

*(*FORTUNETELLER *up into the air, grabs something invisible,*
hands it to PHILIP.*)*

PHILIP: *(Reading the piece of paper)* It's in English.

FORTUNETELLER: No, is in American.

PHILIP: Catherine, this is amazing. *(Reads)* "Say good-bye to Chicago." How'd you know we're from there?

(FORTUNETELLER shrugs. PHILIP pushes CATHERINE forward)

PHILIP: Do hers.

CATHERINE: Philip, this is humiliating.

FORTUNETELLER: *(Grabbing air again, and handing it to her)* Surrender to fate, *Signora.*

CATHERINE: How in the world? Philip, look at this.

PHILIP: Oh, it's just a misspelling and the "L" is really an "I" with the dot connecting.

FORTUNETELLER: No mistake. True fortune.

CATHERINE: *(Reading)* "You will have difficulty overcoming enamels."

PHILIP: That's "enemies." There's a logical explanation for everything in this world.

CATHERINE: Then how do you explain Chicago?

PHILIP: *(Consulting a map)* He heard your accent. *(Looks off and back at his map)* There's the Duomo— let's go up on the roof!

CATHERINE: I'm going to keep this.

PHILIP: How 'bout that—I figured out the map despite the Italian!

CATHERINE: *(To the FORTUNETELLER)* You have no idea how accurate it is. I am having difficulty overcoming enamels.

FORTUNETELLER: Need more luck.

CATHERINE: Oh, no, we can't afford more. *Grazie.*

FORTUNETELLER: No charge. *(Points to center stage floor)* Spin on balls of bull.

PHILIP: I beg your pardon?

FORTUNETELLER: Is tradition in Milan for luck. Spin on balls of bull.

CATHERINE: *(As they study the floor at center stage)* What a beautiful mosaic. Oh, the poor thing. His little testicles are all worn down.

PHILIP: You just spin—how—on your heel?

FORTUNETELLER: *Si. Buona fortuna! (Leaves)*

CATHERINE: *(As PHILIP goes to the bull on the center stage floor.)* No, Philip, don't! Isn't it enough we blew money on gypsy fortunes?

PHILIP: We need all the luck we can get.

CATHERINE: People are looking. It's embarrassing!

PHILIP: They don't know us. As far as they're concerned, we're just tourists. Might as well act like it. *(Strides to center)*

CATHERINE: Oh, hell! I'll see you in the Duomo. *(Starts to leave)*

(Offstage, someone is whistling On Top of Old Smokey.*)*

PHILIP: *(Spinning on his heel)* Catherine, this is for you!

(PHILIP spinning again as CATHERINE disappears through an arch.)

PHILIP: And for me. *(Spinning as the lights begin to fade)* The trip. *(Spinning)* Everything!

(Lighting change as PHILIP leaves, and MARGARET and TOR come through the ungated archway. TOR is whistling, but starts singing as soon as they appear. She is wearing practical traveling attire; he is well-dressed for travel with the incongruous addition of gloves. He limps.)

TOR: *(Singing)* On top of the Duomo
Right here in Milan
I lost my poor lover
When she dove like a swan.

MARGARET: Stop that. We need to be inconspicuous.

TOR: They've never seen us before. We're automatically inconspicuous.

MARGARET: Not with you wearing gloves when it's so warm. And what's with that limp?

TOR: *(Limping)* What limp?

(CATHERINE and PHILIP arrive through the ungated archway. MARGARET nudges TOR for silence and they try to look inconspicuous.)

CATHERINE: You Lutherans miss out on all the fun with saints. That statue was Saint Bartholemew flayed.

PHILIP: So he was holding his skin?

CATHERINE: Wasn't it beautiful? Really just an excuse for an incredible study of anatomy.

PHILIP: Look at that view!

CATHERINE: This is nothing. Wait till you see the view from the Duomo in Florence or Saint Peter's.

(CATHERINE and PHILIP use binoculars and start taking pictures.)

TOR: So, how do you feel?

MARGARET: That's not just a pleasantry?

TOR: We're on top of the Duomo, they've arrived as expected, and I wanna know what you plan to do.

MARGARET: I hadn't really thought. Once it starts happening, I'll know.

TOR: And if nothing happens we can go back to the hotel?

MARGARET: I have a feeling I won't be seeing La Scala.

PHILIP: Every spire has a saint.

CATHERINE: There are a hundred and fifty of them.

MARGARET: What should I say to him?

TOR: Nothing. If it's meant to happen, he'll talk to you first.

MARGARET: You'd put the kibosh on the whole thing!

TOR: *(Sotto voce, but loud enough that* CATHERINE *and* PHILIP *can't help but hear.)* Meg, it's my moral obligation! I'm out of my mind to let you come up here in the first place.

MARGARET: Did you come only to stop me?

TOR: You still think this is just a funny series of coincidences—

MARGARET: It's not coincidence—it's God!

TOR: And you're perfectly safe in the bosom of the Lord.

MARGARET: That's faith, my dear. Something I never fully understood until now.

TOR: *(Taking off his shoes)* God isn't safe.

MARGARET: What are you doing?

TOR: You're not thinking about consequences. I'm showing you some.

MARGARET: Tor, they're looking!

TOR: Maybe they need to see this, too! Maybe that would put a stop to it! *(Throws his shoes offstage)*

MARGARET: *(Running to look over the edge of the roof)* If you hit someone—!

PHILIP: Um...hey!

MARGARET: *(Glancing nervously at* PHILIP*)* Tor, this isn't how it's supposed to happen!

TOR: *(Peeling off his shirt)* How do you know? Maybe this is exactly what's supposed to happen.

PHILIP: Shouldn't somebody stop him? Aren't there guards?

MARGARET: You're provoking—! Please, please, stop!

TOR: *(Gets the shirt off, revealing a small wound in his side)* I'm not provoking, I'm preventing! *(Throws the shirt after the shoes)*

MARGARET: What happened to your side?

TOR: Oh, that's the least of it. *(Pulls off his socks)* My feet, too—hence the limp!

CATHERINE: Philip, he's going to hurt her.

MARGARET: *(Going to her knees to examine his wounded feet)* Tor, what happened?

TOR: *(Pulling off the gloves)* I was hoping you could tell me. I think it's usually a religious phenomenon.

PHILIP: Hey, buddy. Maybe you shouldn't—

TOR: *(Tossing the gloves after the shoes and shirt)* Hey, buddy, maybe *you* shouldn't. You're gonna end up worse than this! *(Displays his wounded palms)*

CATHERINE: My God! Stigmata! *(She takes a flash picture.)*

MARGARET: Oh, Tor!

PHILIP: Um...isn't this the kinda private thing you might wanna do somewhere else?

MARGARET: *(To* PHILIP*)* I'm not ready! I'm not ready for you!

PHILIP: What? I'm sorry—

MARGARET: Tor, you forced this—!

TOR: I'm trying to stop it!

CATHERINE: Our first day in Italy and already we're witnessing a miracle. *(She takes a picture.)*

MARGARET: Go to Rome! Whatever happens, make sure you go to Rome!

PHILIP: Why?

MARGARET: There's no time! I can't tell you! There's never any time! But that's where you'll find what you're looking for.

CATHERINE: How do you know what he's looking for? He doesn't even know.

PHILIP: Catherine, please, don't start—

MARGARET: That's why the throne is empty. We're the judges! We decide. We judge *ourselves.*

PHILIP: What empty throne?

MARGARET: Please just tell me this: Why choose the pain of martyrdom over the pain of life?

PHILIP: Martyrdom?

(TOR whistles the Jeopardy *theme.)*

PHILIP: I'm sorry, ma'am—I don't—

CATHERINE: Because it's holy!

MARGARET: I want your answer!

PHILIP: Because martyrdom's...shorter. It's over more quickly.

MARGARET: Of course! I knew you'd say that!

CATHERINE: Philip, what an awful thing to say!

MARGARET: That's his answer! His faith reverses mine, like a mirror! That's why you have to go to Rome. *(She*

kisses him.) I love you, Philip. I'm sorry, Catherine.
Tor, forgive me.

TOR: Meg, no—stay away from the edge—!

PHILIP: What's she doing?

*(*MARGARET *dodges* TOR *and runs through the gated archway, slamming the gate behind her. He leaps to the gate.*

TOR: It's locked! Where does this go?

PHILIP: *(As they look high upstage, then turn to look high above the audience.)* Up...to...

CATHERINE: The top of the cupola.

PHILIP: The highest part.

TOR: Catherine, you know Italian—call a guard or the police or someone!

CATHERINE: How do you know I know Italian?

TOR: Call!

CATHERINE: *Gendarme! Gendarme!*

PHILIP: Sweetheart, that's French.

CATHERINE: Oh, of course. *Aiuto! Carabinieri! Polizia!*

PHILIP: *(Pointing up over the audience)* There she is!

TOR: Meg! No!

CATHERINE: *Aiuto!*

PHILIP: Please, ma'am! You could fall!

TOR: You can call her Margaret. Believe me.

PHILIP: Margaret, whatever is bothering you, come down so we can talk about it.

TOR: What if it's all lies? A trick!?

PHILIP: Why is she doing this?

TOR: She thinks God wants her to jump.

CATHERINE: Margaret! Sometimes Satan disguises himself as God!

PHILIP: Thou shalt not tempt the Lord your God!

MILANESE POLICEMAN: *(Rushing in) Cosa é tutto questo gridare? ("What is all this shouting?")*

CATHERINE: Oh, *mille grazie. ("A thousand thanks." Pointing) Questa donna—she wants to jump— (Mimes jumping)*

MILANESE POLICEMAN: *Dov'e? Non vedo niente. ("Where is she? I don't see anything.")*

CATHERINE: *(Points and uses binoculars)* She's right there, right next to Saint—Lucy—I think—cause that looks like a dish of eyeballs—

MARGARET: *(Off and above)* Philip, do you love me?

TOR: No—tell her no!

PHILIP: I don't even know her! But if she's depressed—!

TOR: If you tell her yes, she'll jump.

PHILIP: If I tell her no, that might be what pushes her over the edge. I know about depression.

CATHERINE: Tell her yes, Philip. Tell her you love her. It might be the only thing that can save her.

TOR: *(Trying the locked gate. To the* MILANESE POLICEMAN*)* Do you have the key? How do you say key?

CATHERINE: *Chiave.*

TOR: *Chiave? Chiave!?*

MILANESE POLICEMAN: *(Pulling* TOR *away from the gate) No, no! Passaggio vietato! ("Passage forbidden!")*

CATHERINE: *(Gives a little scream)* Philip, tell her! She's about to—! She's about to—!

PHILIP: Margaret, I love you! Can you hear me!
I love you!

CATHERINE: Philip! She's smiling!

(CATHERINE *screams as they see* MARGARET *jump.*)

TOR: Meg!!

PHILIP: No!!

(Their eyes follow MARGARET's *plummet, but after only
a few seconds, they gasp. Their gaze arrests in mid-descent,
then slowly rises.)*

CATHERINE: Oh, my God.

PHILIP: That's impossible.

TOR: It's true. It's all true.

MILANESE POLICEMAN: *Cosa? Che cos'e?* ("What?
What is it?")

PHILIP: She's floating.

CATHERINE: She's ascending.

TOR: Just like you said.

PHILIP: Who said?

TOR: You did.

(CATHERINE *and* PHILIP *look at* TOR, *puzzled, but before
they can say anything, they are distracted by a bright golden
light emanating from above the audience. The light shines
on* CATHERINE, PHILIP *and* TOR, *but not on the* MILANESE
POLICEMAN. CATHERINE *puts on sunglasses.)*

PHILIP: *(As the three of them squint)* What's that?

TOR: God rays.

CATHERINE: I can barely see her.

MILANESE POLICEMAN: *Signora, che cos'e fa?* ("Signora,
what's happening?")

(With a clink, a ring drops down from above. CATHERINE, *the* MILANESE POLICEMAN *and* PHILIP *jump back, but* TOR *is unperturbed.)*

CATHERINE: She's throwing money!

TOR: No, it's just a ring. Pick it up. *(To* PHILIP, *who picks up the ring)* It's for you.

PHILIP: I've never seen anything like this.

CATHERINE: Shhh! She's saying something.

MARGARET: *(Voice. Very far off.)* I can see La Scala from here!

*(*TOR *starts whistling* The Hallelujah Chorus *as their gaze continues upward.)*

MILANESE POLICEMAN: *(To* TOR*)* Signore, dove sono i Suoi vestiti? E nudo, Lei! ("Where are you clothes? You're indecent!") (To all three of them) Temo di dovervi chiedervi d'andare via. Spaventate gli altri turisti. ("I'm afraid I'll have to ask you to leave. You're frightening the other tourists.")

CATHERINE: Philip, we should go.

PHILIP: But...she's—

CATHERINE: Do you want to spend our whole trip in a Milanese police station?

TOR: No, don't go! There's so much to explain.

(When TOR *stops whistling to speak, other offstage whistlers quietly harmonize the tune.)*

PHILIP: Yes, there is! What the hell is going on in this country?!

MILANESE POLICEMAN: *(To* TOR.*)* Passaporto, per favore. ("Passport, please.")

CATHERINE: Philip, we can't get too involved.

TOR: It's way, way too late.

CATHERINE: *(Tugging at him)* Philip, he's weird.
I'm feeling anxious.

PHILIP: But...I want to know—that woman—!

CATHERINE: Please!

TOR: If you'll just listen, I can save you so much—

CATHERINE: No! Come on!

PHILIP: *(As* CATHERINE *drags him through the ungated arch.)* I'm sorry—!

*(*TOR *turns back to the glow emanating from above and hears the other whistlers. He joins them in whistling the* Chorus. *The* MILANESE POLICEMAN *stares into the sky, seeing nothing, then turns back to* TOR.*)*

MILANESE POLICEMAN: *Passaporto, Signore, per favore.*

*(*TOR *begins to conduct the heavenly whistling chorus, a beatific smile on his face. The whistling grows louder as the lights fade.)*

MILANESE POLICEMAN: *Signore? Passaporto?*

(Blackout)

END OF PLAY

·

www.ingramcontent.com/pod-product-compliance
Lightning Source LLC
Chambersburg PA
CBHW070023110426
42741CB00034B/2442